Egbert Coffin Smyth

Recent Excavations in Ancient Christian Cemeteries

Egbert Coffin Smyth

Recent Excavations in Ancient Christian Cemeteries

ISBN/EAN: 9783337258993

Printed in Europe, USA, Canada, Australia, Japan

Cover: Foto ©ninafisch / pixelio.de

More available books at **www.hansebooks.com**

RECENT EXCAVATIONS

IN

ANCIENT CHRISTIAN CEMETERIES.

[From the Proceedings of the American Antiquarian Society, New Series, Vol. II, Part I., April 26, 1882.]

BY

EGBERT C. SMYTH.

WORCESTER:
PRESS OF CHARLES HAMILTON,
311 MAIN STREET.
1882.

NOTE.

The paper on " Recent Excavations in Ancient Christian Cemeteries" was written as a part of the Report of the Council of the American Antiquarian Society, and for convenience, the entire report is here given. The treatment of the special subject begins at page 8.

ANCIENT CHRISTIAN CEMETERIES.

In presenting its semi-annual Report, the Council gratefully recognizes that, with the completion of the year, this Society will have reached the good old age of three-score years and ten, and that its promise of continued strength and augmented usefulness never was brighter.

The report of Mr. Nathaniel Paine, our Treasurer, will give a satisfactory exhibit of our funds. The Society will notice with peculiar interest that Mrs. Haven, in her sympathy with her husband's kindness to the association, has paid, earlier than was required, his legacy of one thousand dollars; and has added her personal gifts of a tasteful Brussels carpet, and Mr. Haven's closed desk.

The Assistant-Librarian, Mr. Edmund M. Barton, reports an active use of the Library, and an unusual increase in the last six months. The receipts were,—of books, one thousand and forty-seven volumes; of pamphlets, four thousand eight hundred and ninety-six; of bound newspapers, twenty volumes; of unbound newspapers, one hundred and twenty-two volumes. The gifts were from two hundred and sixteen sources, viz. :—from forty-eight members, from one hundred and seven friends, and from sixty-one Societies and Institutions. Valuable additions have been made to the Isaac Davis alcove of Spanish-American books.

The Society will hear with especial pleasure that our associate, Professor E. D. Salisbury, of New Haven, has presented to it one of the few bronze copies of the beautiful gold medal presented last February by the Yale professors to Ex-President Woolsey, in commemoration of the fiftieth anniversary of his connection with the College.

Professor Dwight, of New Haven, has characterised President Woolsey's administration as carrying "the scholarly life of the College * * * to a far higher development than ever before. * * * The love of learning for learning's sake, and the glory and beauty of its adornments to a cultivated mind became in a higher sense than ever the inspiring power of all within the circle of the institution. A noble example stood in full vision before all eyes, of a Christian scholar, hating all deception and pretence, holding up the standard of thorough truthfulness of feeling and purpose in every kind of intellectual and moral effort." By his published writings on International Law, Political Science, Communism, Divorce; by his presidency of one of the largest and most useful of our benevolent societies; and by his active participation in the labors of the Revisers of King James's version of our New Testament, Dr. Woolsey has exerted a pure and powerful influence on the discussion of the greatest themes, and in the development of the social and religious life of nations. The medal so appropriately presented to him, "was struck," it is said, "in France, is massive gold, and over six inches in circumference, having a weight * * * of six ounces Troy. On the face it carries the inscription: ' *Suo Preceptori, Preceptores Collegii Yalensis,* 1831–1881,' and on the obverse the head of President Woolsey in profile, with his name in the border. A number of bronze copies were struck, whose value will be enhanced by the accident which befel the die after the one hundredth was struck."[1]

On Friday, March 31, a party of Zuñi Indians, accompanied by the Rev. Dr. E. E. Hale, and Mr. Frank H. Cushing, of the ethnological department of the Smithsonian Institution, visited Worcester chiefly for the purpose of seeing the prehistoric relics from Central America gathered in the hall of this Society, "there being a hope that they might find among them something analogous to their own legendary history." A very interesting account of this visit, and of their recep-

---

[1] *The Independent*, Feb. 23, 1882.

tion at the Hall by the President and other members of
the Society, as well as of their sojourn in Worcester, was
published in the *Evening Gazette* of that city, for March
31 and April 1. This Society has already printed a
learned Essay from Prof. Henry W. Haynes,[*] who favors
the claim of the Zuñi pueblos to be regarded as the true site
of " The Seven Cities of Cibola ;" and there is reason to hope
that through Mr. Cushing facts respecting the ancient history
of this people, and customs of great interest in themselves
and in their connections with other researches, will be made
known.

It is our painful duty to record the removal from us
by death during the past six months of four of our associates.
On December 1, 1881, Hon. Solomon Lincoln died, aged
seventy-seven years and four months. He was elected to
this Society in October, 1861, and was a cordial and
respected member. He was a native of Hingham, and a
resident there at the time of his death. Graduating at
Brown University in 1822, having as classmates Rev.
Alexis Caswell, LL.D., and Hon. Isaac Davis, he taught
a grammar school for a few months and then pursued the
study of law, receiving admission to the bar November
21, 1826. He represented the town of Hingham at the
General Court in 1829 and 1840, and was a member of
the Senate in 1830 and 1831. Beside these and other
offices, he held various important local trusts, and was
a very frequent contributor to various public journals.
He had a taste for local history, for genealogical studies,
for relics of antiquity, and found time from his profes-
sional and public duties to write the history of Hingham,
"a lasting monument to his memory." Several historical
orations delivered by him were published, and also "An
Historical sketch of Nantasket," "Notes on the Lincoln
Families of Massachusetts, with some account of the Family

---

[*] Proceedings, Oct. 21, 1881, p. 421, sq.

2

of Abraham Lincoln," and a "Memoir of the Rev. Charles Brooks."[1]

December 17, 1881, Hon. Lewis H. Morgan, LL.D., died at his home in Rochester, N. Y., aged seventy-three years and twenty-six days. He became a member of this Society in 1865. He was one of the foremost ethnological scholars and authors of this country, and most abundant in labors for the promotion of historical learning. This Society gloried in its association with him, and deeply mourns its loss in his death.

January 10, 1882, one of the most gentle, true, brave and beloved of men, Delano A. Goddard, Esq., was taken away. Elected a member October, 1880, he actively exhibited his taste and ability for the special duties which he thus assumed. From a rapid sketch that has been published of his life, a few facts may be taken for this occasion.[2] He was born in Worcester, August 27, 1831, and inherited from his parents strong convictions, a love of truth and justice, and fine literary tastes. He graduated at Yale in 1853, and began his career as a journalist in Painesville, Ohio. After a service of about a year he came to Boston, and was connected with the *Chronicle*, which was not long afterwards merged with the *Telegraph*, and subsequently with the *Traveller*. In 1857, he returned to Worcester, was associated for awhile with Mr. Hooper on the *Evening Transcript* (afterwards the *Gazette*), and then was connected with the *Spy*, becoming associate Editor. In 1868, he joined the editorial corps of the *Daily Advertiser*, in this city, and in a few months succeeded Mr. Charles F. Dunbar, as Editor-in-chief. His character and career as a journalist are worthy of being kept in perpetual remembrance. From the manifold duties and cares of his responsible position, he found leisure to make several contributions of permanent

---

[1] An obituary notice, and partial list of his publications, was given in the *Hingham Journal*, December 9, 1881.

[2] *Boston Daily Advertiser*, January 11, 1882.

value to our historical literature—particularly in the chapters he wrote for the "Memorial History of Boston."

Among the tributes to his useful life, none are more pathetic than the speeches made at a council of the Omaha Indians, summoned on receipt of the news of his death ; and next to the evidence of their gratitude, the most touching fact in all that was said or done was this : they never mentioned his name. Like his Master—it has been fittingly remarked—he " made himself of no reputation."

Time would fail us to speak as we would of our eminent associate, Hon. Alexander H. Bullock, LL.D., who departed this life suddenly, January 17, 1882, aged sixty-five years, ten months and fifteen days. He was elected a member of this Society in April, 1855, served as Recording Secretary from 1858 to 1861, and frequently took part in its proceedings. Very vivid in our recollections is his admirable address, published in the Proceedings of the Society, on the Centennial of the Massachusetts Constitution,—a paper of permanent value.

From a review of his life published in one of the journals of the city of which he was the pride, we learn of his strong New England ancestry, of his admission to Amherst College at the early age of sixteen (he was born March 2, 1816), of his graduating with the salutatory oration, of his study of the law at Harvard, under Judge Story, and in the office of Hon. Emory Washburn, of Worcester, of his admission to the bar in 1841, of his services in both branches of the Legislature of Massachusetts, of his engaging in journalism, of his returning to public life—first, as Mayor of Worcester, then, in the Legislature where he became Speaker of the House, and the warm and influential supporter of Governor Andrew, whom he succeeded in the Gubernatorial chair.

He was made a Doctor of Laws both by Harvard and Amherst, in 1865. Beside his official papers, as a leading member of the Legislature, and as Governor, his orations and addresses on many important public occasions secure for him a place among the eminent citizens and orators of this Commonwealth, and of our nation.

It should be added that the Council met on announcement of Gov. Bullock's decease and passed Resolutions in his honor, and with other members of the Society attended his funeral. [1]

Although the main object of this Society is to promote the study of American antiquities, it has not been unusual at its meetings to consider archæological investigations in other lands. Our memories are still as fresh as delightful of the account which our honored President gave of the discoveries at Hissarlik, and of their significance in respect to the Homeric story of the fall of ancient Troy. On the present occasion, the writer of the remainder of this report —for which he alone is responsible—is permitted to turn your thoughts to recent excavations in ancient Christian cemeteries, particularly those in the vicinity of Rome—the *novum Ilium*—whose buried treasures, through their connection with the early story of the Christian faith and its martyr heroes, have for us a yet deeper interest than any remains of classic antiquity.

Neander's "General History of the Christian Church," contains, it has been said, no allusion to the Catacombs, and it makes but little account of Christian Inscriptions.

---

[1] Notice was taken in the report, of the death of another member of the Society, Rev. Sidney Harper Marsh, D.D., President of Pacific University, Forest Grove, Oregon. It appears from a memorial written by Rev. Mr. Eells, that he was born August 29, 1825, and died February 2, 1879. His father's family were distinguished for learning and influence, and his mother was a grand-daughter, or (more probably) a great grand-daughter of Rev. Dr. Eleazer Wheelock, the founder and first President of Dartmouth College. His life-work was similar to that of his respected ancestor, and he is highly commended for similar qualifications and satisfactory results. He was elected a member of the American Antiquarian Society in October, 1860, but his devoted service to his College, under special difficulties, left him no power for the antiquarian and historical work that was expected from his talents and learning.

It would be impossible for this most eminent historian, were he living to-day, to avoid an abundant use of the new materials which recent discoveries in these cemeteries have brought to light. It is no exaggeration to say, that new chapters in the history of the Christian Church are now unfolding, new traces of its progress, new and multiplied and important facts for the interpretation of its constitution, its doctrine, its ritual, its life. The work indeed is only begun, and it proceeds with a deplorable slowness. Of eighty or more Christian burial-places, known to be of very great antiquity, scarcely one-half have been suitably studied. Only about ten have been excavated with any approach to thoroughness.[1] In the immediate vicinity of Rome, some forty important Catacombs still remain either to be properly identified, or to be completely excavated. Remarkable and abundant as have been the results of De Rossi's labors, his *magnum opus*, in three large quarto volumes, treats, with an unimportant exception, of but one group of Catacombs. Only two other cemeteries, of the whole large number, have been excavated during the last twenty years, although the attention of scholars has been generally and earnestly turned to the progress of this work. Meanwhile there are many cemeteries and private burial-places beside the Roman, of which enough is known greatly to stimulate curiosity, but which are almost wholly neglected—ancient tombs in Syria and Asia Minor, in Alexandria and Cyrene, in Milos and Syracuse, in Naples and other places in Italy. "The Catacombs of the leading churches of the East," says a cautious German archæologist, to whom we are greatly indebted, "are not yet discovered. That they exist, cannot be doubted."[2]

While we thus regret that more is not accomplished, we would not fail to recognize how much has been achieved.

---

[1] Victor Schulze: Zeitschrift für Kirch. Wissensch. XII., 1881, p. 648.
[2] Schulze, l. c., p. 648.

Some fifteen thousand Inscriptions have already been obtained from Catacombs, of which twelve thousand at least are from the Roman. Innumerable objects illustrative of primitive Christian customs and life have been collected and studied. Above all, a scientific method of investigation has been substituted for the zeal of dogmatists and relic hunters. Exploration of the Catacombs, it has well been said, is becoming equivalent to a scientific knowledge of the monumental sources of early Christian history. Especially has an exact topographical method been applied to the study of the Roman Catacombs. The utmost pains have been taken to trace their development. Their chronology has been investigated with gratifying results. The growth, for example, of St. Callistus, with its adjuncts, has been traced so that a distinct and accurate record of its successive stages can be traced from about the close of the second century, through the period of persecutions, and down to the fifth century. Great progress, also, has been made in the chronology and the interpretation of the pictures of the Catacombs—a branch of the subject more fruitful than any other for the student of the thoughts and spirit of the early Christians. The rapidly growing literature of the subject is an indication of the value of the results obtained. Since the Rev. Dr. James Freeman Clarke delivered his valuable Lowell lectures on the Roman Catacombs, in which he alludes to the principal writers on this subject, Monsieur Theophile Roller has published an accurate and copious illustrated folio of seven hundred and thirty-one pages ; and the German scholar to whom allusion has just been made, has informed us, while this report is preparing, of an elaborate work in press from his own pen. Numerous essays are also beginning to appear from writers who are popularizing the materials collected by various investigators.

Good Bishop Burnet, who visited Rome in 1685, about half a century after the publication of Bosio's *Roma Sot-*

teránea, contended that the Catacombs were not the work
of the primitive Christians, but were the common burying-
places of the ancient heathen; "that the mountains of
rubbish thrown out would betray the Christians to their
enemies;" that assemblies for worship there would have
been impossible on account of the decay of so many bodies;
that "the number of Christians at Rome was insufficient for
such a gigantic work." He adds: "I am as little subject
to vapors as most men, yet I had all the day long after I
was in them, which was not near an hour, a confusion, and
as it were, a boiling in my head, that disordered me
extremely;" and "this inexhaustible magazine of bones,
which, by all appearance, are no other than the bones of
the Pagan Romans, supplies the Papacy with relics which
are now sent over the world to feed a superstition that is
as blind as it proves expensive." Dr. Lundy, from whose
ingenious work on "Monumental Christianity," we take
these extracts, adds: "Perhaps it was the Papacy itself
that made his head boil."

However this may be, the Bishop's comments show
how poor a guide to archæological investigations is
dogmatic or ecclesiastical prejudice, for the results of
scientific investigations evince that the Bishop was wrong
in every particular, unless we except the expensiveness
of relics and the confusion or boiling sensation in his
head.

The Roman Catacombs are now proved to be, for the
most part, the work of the early Christians. That they did
not originate the idea of rock-hewn sepulchres, or of subterranean chambers and galleries, the tombs of Etruria, and
similar Pagan monuments on the Appian Way, at once
suggest. Probably the Jewish Catacomb near the same
street and still others are older than the introduction of
Christianity to Rome. Yet the numerous and vast cemeteries of which we are speaking, it is now acknowledged,
are neither of Pagan nor Jewish creation, but were originally

excavated for members of the Christian Church at Rome or their fellow-disciples from other similar communions.[1]

Another assured result of recent studies is, that down at least to the year 257, the date of an edict by Valerian, forbidding Dionysius, bishop of Rome, and "any others," "either to hold conventions or to enter what you call your cemeteries," the Christians of that city, except in rare and brief seasons, could prosecute undisturbed the work of excavation, and could bury and commemorate their dead with appropriate solemnities.

The Roman laws were exceedingly protective of all burial places and burial rites. At first, Christianity was sheltered under the toleration extended to Judaism. Then, private persons having landed property in the vicinity of the city, could set apart areas for burial purposes, and open them to whomsoever they pleased. Then, as the Christian community increased, cemeteries owned by the church and completely under its control could be legally held under the laws for burial associations. As the Roman State grew more and more conscious of the deadly antagonism between itself, in its religious theory and practice, and the new religion—still called new by a writer of the second

---

[1] In response to a question from Rev. Dr. Ellis the following reasons were given for the general abandonment by recent authorities of the theory once universally held, viz., that the early Christians simply used, for burial purposes, exhausted *arenariæ:* (1) The Christian Catacombs are almost entirely excavated in the *tufa granolare*, and carefully avoid the *tufa friabile* from which chiefly sand was obtained for mortar and cement; (2) The Christian cemeteries are characterized by numerous narrow galleries, crossing each other at right angles, and evidently planned so as to secure the greatest amount of wall for *loculi*, whereas the sand-pits exhibit broad, curved cart tracks, constructed so as to obtain with greatest facility the largest quantity of *pozzolana*. Sometimes everything is removed save the requisite support for the roof. The visitor in passing, as at the Catacomb of Priscilla, from an *arenaria* to a Catacomb is struck at once with the change in construction. See Northcote & Brownlow; *Roma Sotteranea* I., p. 375 sq.; *Dict. of Chr. Antiq.* I., p. 295 sq.; Herzog & Plitt, *Real-Encyclopädie*, VII., p. 559 · Roller, *Les Catacombes de Rome*, I., p. XIII. sq.

and third centuries—it was naturally less and less tolerant of what before had been winked at, viz., that the cemeteries were powerful allies of the church, that the sainted dead were inspirers of living Christians, that the burial club was a Christian Church which it was a necessity of the State to suppress and even exterminate. But this was not realized for long, and so for generations, save in times of special excitement, the Christians were able peacefully to lay away their dead, and duly to honor the places of sacred rest. The query may arise why, if there was this tranquillity, subterranean vaults should have been constructed at so great cost of labor. There are allusions in early writers to cemeteries in certain localities in the open air. · If any such existed at Rome before the fourth century no traces of them have been discovered. The habit of burial at Rome as generally in the East was in family tombs. The church was a larger family. Nothing is more fully brought to evidence than this intense feeling of fraternity. It broke down all social distinctions, all limitations of rank, tribe, nation. The Christian tie was stronger than that of blood. The rich opened their burial areas to the poor. The men and women in whose veins may have flowed the blood of the Flavian dynasty, or of the Cornelii, or the Cæcilii, or the Pretextati, or the senatorial house of Pudens, enlarged their sepulchres not only for their relatives and dependents, but for their fellow-disciples. The church grew beyond what history has recorded or believed. · Men came into it from every nation. Brethren from distant churches were received with Christian hospitality, and if death overtook them at Rome, their bodies were tenderly laid away in the Christian cemeteries. Large cemeteries in the open air, sufficiently near the city to be accessible, would have required extensive purchases of land. The tufa of the hills, soft enough to be easily worked, firm enough to admit of galleries with comparatively thin walls, and of successive stories, one beneath another, as deep as could be excavated without reaching water, admitted of compact burial places, for immense numbers. Then too, from the beginning, or at least from the time of Trajan, the services which Christians would naturally use in connection with interments, or in commemoration of the departed, would often be impracticable in the open air, in the midst of a hostile and easily excited population. At last even these subterranean retreats were no protection. But with rare and late exceptions their privacy would enable Christian friends to follow the customs of their faith in comparative seclusion and without provocation to the votaries of other and hostile religions.

Whatever the explanation, the fact is assured that from at least the second century—perhaps from an earlier date— Christian burial at Rome was in these under-ground cemeteries. And there are no indications to suggest a doubt that this was the exclusive practice throughout the period of persecutions.

Interments in the Catacombs seem to have substantially ceased after the first decade of the fifth century. Recent discoveries have revealed extensive cemeteries above ground, one immediately over the catacomb of St. Callistus, with dated inscriptions going back to the year 358, possibly 337, and continuing to about the middle of the sixth century. After 364, and for the remainder of the century, two out of three burials, apparently, were above ground. Supposing that Christianity was introduced to Rome soon after the day of Pentecost we should have, at the most, about ten generations, in full, and about the equivalent of another, occupying these subterranean cemeteries. Some margin, how large cannot be definitely stated, yet not sufficient seriously to disturb our calculation, must be admitted for later burials. Assuming then that these Catacombs are the work of about eleven generations their extent is surprising. Michel de Rossi, brother of the distinguished explorer and author, a "practical mathematician," has estimated that the galleries of the cemeteries within a radius of three miles from Rome amount in length to at least 559 miles. Others give a much higher estimate. It is calculated that one four-hundredth of a square mile would allow space for galleries three-fifths of a mile in length, on a single level. Constructing with an average of two stories in depth, this small superficial space would admit of galleries a mile and one fifth in extent. In the single crypt of Lucina, whose entire area is 100 by 230 feet, and only very partially used, so far as known by excavation, De Rossi counted over 700 *loculi*, and estimated that nearly twice this number had been destroyed, giving a total of 2000. The most careful statement so far made allows for nearly 4,000,000 separate graves. Others give numbers as high as six or even seven millions. The discrepancy shows that the calculation is still largely conjectural. It must be admitted that without further excavation no precise numbers can be given. But at the lowest probable estimate, that of De Rossi, the extent of line is enormous; and the number of graves indicates, after all reasonable deductions are made for the burial of strangers, a much larger Christian population at Rome than history has made account of.[1] Tacitus's expression, *ingens multitudo*, must early have become a literal fact.

The interpreters of De Rossi to English readers, Messrs. Northcote and Brownlow, claim with confidence that the chronology of several catacombs can be carried back to the Apostolic Age. Those for which such high antiquity is claimed are the crypts of the Vatican; the catacomb of St. Paul on the Ostian way; of Priscilla (supposed by some to be the mother of Pudens, a Roman Senator), on the Via Salaria Nova; the Ostian cemetery, where the Apostle Peter is said to have baptized; and the cemetery of Domitilla on the Via Ardeatina, where, according to tradition, were buried

---

[1] Rawlinson assumes 7,000,000 of graves; then says that such a number in, say, 400 years time, give an average population of from 500,000 to 700,000. Total population of Rome, 1,500,000 to 2,000,000 at beginning of Empire.

her two chamberlains, Nereus and Achilleus, and also Petronilla, whom legend transformed into a daughter of St. Peter.
Two or three others are sometimes added; but those just
mentioned are the most important, and the claim preferred
for them is gaining credence.[1]

Let us examine for a moment the state of the evidence.

The claim for the crypts of the Vatican rests chiefly on
the supposed discovery of an epitaph bearing the name
Linus, one of the earliest overseers or bishops of the
Church of Rome. But the accounts of this inscription are
contradictory, and the whole matter does not as yet amount
to plausible conjecture.

Something more can be said for the existence, in the first
century, of a cemetery on the Ostian Way where the Apostle
Paul is said to have been buried. Yet the evidence is not
decisive, and the cutting away of the hill in which interments seem to have been made has probably destroyed the
possibility of arriving at any certainty. The graves of
Peter and Paul Providence has probably made as uncertain
as that of Moses.

In the year 1873, a crypt was discovered near St. Agnes
for which De Rossi had long been in search—the cemetery
named in mediæval writings as the Ostian, as the *cœmeterium
fontis beati Petri*, as *ad nymphas ubi Petrus baptizaverat*,
as *ad Emerentianam* and as possessing a *cathedra*, the first
seat from which Peter preached. A place so intimately associated with Peter, it is obvious, has peculiar attractions for
Roman Catholics so devout as De Rossi and his English
interpreters, and we may not wonder if the discoveries actu-
ally made have seemed to them of greater significance than
a cooler criticism can allow. The newly discovered crypt
contains a chair cut in the tufa. An inscription also has
been found which reads SANCPE . . . CEMERENTIANE—
which is restored so as to read SANCTus PEtrus. SANCTA
EMERENTIANE. The inscriptions and chair show us per-

---

[1] See Appendix, Note A.

haps traditions or legends of the sixth, possibly of the fourth and fifth centuries, but cannot claim for themselves a higher antiquity. Yet it is quite possible, and indeed not improbable, that this discovery reveals one of the earliest Christian cemeteries. A number of marbles with inscriptions which might well have been written within the first century had long been known and been believed to be from this lost Christian cemetery. The new discovery confirms this belief, presenting others still *in situ*, some few of them "marked with a Christian symbol." Yet here again we cannot be sure of our dates. They may have been cut any time in the first third of the second century, as well as in the last third of the first. It is, in any event, a fact of deep interest that we are carried back so far.

The cemetery of Priscilla has very recently been more thoroughly excavated in the hope and expectation of discovering evidences of its origin in the apostolic age—but without success. The Greek chapel, as it is called, which has been supposed to be the nucleus of the cemetery, cannot be proved to be earlier than the second century, and no epitaph, or other indication, has been found confirmatory of the tradition that the cemetery was "dug in the property of the family of Pudens converted by the Apostles." This may be so, but at present we must be content to stop where the evidence does, at some point, perhaps a very early one, in the second century, however strongly we may hope that the possibilities of further information are not exhausted.

One other of the more important cemeteries for which an origin in apostolic times is claimed is that of Domitilla, or of Nereus and Achilleus, or of Petronilla—as sometimes designated. The discoveries here are very remarkable, and prove a very high antiquity.

Historians of every school from Gibbon to the present time have inferred from statements made by early non-Christian writers, and by Eusebius, that Titus Flavius Clemens, nephew of Vespasian, cousin to Domitian, and

4

consul in the year 95, became a Christian and suffered martyrdom. His wife, Flavia Domitilla, grand-daughter or great grand-daughter of Vespasian, also appears to have espoused the same faith, and to have been banished therefor. According to tradition as preserved in the apocryphal Acts of Nereus and Achilleus, two of her chamberlains, just named, were put to death and buried in a crypt, in land belonging to their mistress, a mile and a half from the city, on the Ardeatine way, "near a sepulchre where had been interred Petronilla, daughter of the Apostle Peter."

In a list of the Roman cemeteries found in a manuscript of the ninth century, the name of Domitilla is associated with those of Nereus and Achilleus, and with that of Petronilla—*Domitillæ, Nerei et Achillei, ad s. Petronillam, via Ardeatina.*[1]

Some excavations made by the Duchess dello Sciablese, in the year 1817, brought to light the following inscription :

SER · CORNELIO
IVLIANO FRAT.
PIISSIMO ET
CAL *vis* AE · EIVS
P. CALVISIVS
PHILO*t*AS · ET · SIBI
EX INDVLGENTIA
FLAVIAE DOMITILL—
IN FR · P · XXXV
IN AGR. P. XXXX,

Showing that an area large enough for the beginning of a Catacomb, viz., 35 feet in front and 40 deep—was granted by permission of Flavia Domitilla. Another inscription had been found in 1772, containing the words, FLAVIAE · DOMITILLae VESPASIANI · NEPTIS · · · BENEFICIO. There is nothing to indicate whether these inscrip-

---

[1] Cf. *Mommsen* in *Cont. Rev.*, 1871, p. 169; De Rossi, *Bulletino di Archeologia Cristiana*, 1874, p. 6; *Rom. Sott.*, I. p. 266; Parker, *Arch. of Rome*, pt. xii. p. 161.

tions are Christian or pagan. They simply prove—taken by themselves—that Flavia Domitilla, grand-daughter of Vespasian, owned and granted land where is now a catacomb.

De Rossi had supposed this Catacomb to be that of Callistus, a cemetery known to have been under the control of the church of Rome toward the close of the second century. De Rossi discovered the true Callistan burial-place elsewhere, and suspected the one we are considering to be the cemetery described in the MS. as *coemeterium Domitillœ, Nerei et Achillei, ad Sanctam Petronillam, via Ardeatina.* Petronilla, he saw, cannot be a derivative from Petrus. He proposed another origin. The father of Flavius Clemens, and brother of Vespasian, was Titus Flavius Sabinus, and his grand-father, Titus Flavius Petro. Petronilla is a name naturally borne by a female descendant of Petro.

In 1865, excavations brought to light an entrance to this Catacomb, and a vault whose architectural structure, in the judgment of Mr. Parker, a good authority upon such a point, may be as early as the time of Nero. All the indications are that it was at first a "private burial-place for the founder and his nearest relations. The entrance to the later Catacombs," says Theodor Mommsen, the historian, "though not exactly concealed, is shown as little as possible; a modest opening generally leads by a step into the proper burial-place, and inscriptions are never found except in the inner chambers. Here, on the contrary, the grave is closed on the outside with doors, over which the epitaph was at one time legible. The passages are wide, the vaulted roofs and walls covered with stucco, essentially different from the narrow galleries—generally rough-hewn—of the ordinary Catacombs. But what is peculiarly noteworthy is this, that in the original part of this vault the stone beds, which peculiarly belong to the later Catacombs, do not appear at all. On the other hand, great niches are excavated in the walls for the reception of sarcophagi. At a later time narrower passages were certainly broken through the walls,

and stone beds in their side walls; but, as if clearly to
mark the transition, these stone beds are here surrounded
with a cornice, which gives them the form of sarcophagi.
The remains of the frescoes, which clearly are of the same
time as the original building, are the sole proof that this
grave did not belong to any of those heathens who abstained
from burning, but that it was really from the beginning a
Christian foundation. They are, especially in the mere
ornaments, of rare beauty, and no decorative artist of the
Augustan age need be ashamed of the vaulted roof, particularly with its exquisite garlands of grapes and the birds
pecking at them, and the winged boys gathering and press-
ing out the fruit. There are also small landscapes, which
are never found in the later Christian graves. The groups
drawn on the side walls are less perfect. Among those
still preserved, the most remarkable are Daniel standing
between two lions, the Good Shepherd, Noah's Ark, with
the dove, and the representation of a supper, which differs,
on the whole, but little from the usual antique treatment of
the subject. Two men are represented sitting on the dinner
sofa, before them the round table covered with meats, and
by it the serving slave, yet clearly showing the Christian
influence in the bread placed round the fish on the dish."[3]

In the winter and spring of 1873–4, came new discoveries.
Near the ancient entrance of which we have been speaking,
the excavations uncovered a Basilica which all Rome, and
the strangers therein, went out to see. It was about
100 x 60 feet in dimensions, and so far as can be inferred
from the present state of the walls, about twenty-three feet
high. Its pavement was on a level with the second story
of the cemetery. It seems to have been built in the fourth
or fifth century, and was the place where Gregory the Great
preached a Homily which has come down to our time.[4] It
was called the Basilica of Petronilla, and not only explained

---

Contemp. Rev., 1871, pp. 170–1.   See Appendix, Note B.
[3] Hom., 28.

the old designations, *Coemeterium Domitillæ, Nerei et Achillei, ad Petronillam,* but confirmed the theory as to the names of the Catacombs around and beneath it. More specific indications soon came to light. Fragments were found of a Damasine inscription commemorative of Nereus and Achilleus, of which Mr. Northcote gives a translation ; first recalling, by way of explanation of the allusion in the first lines, that "it was one of Nero's crimes that he employed some of his soldiers, his own body-guard, to be the executioners of his unjust sentences." [1] The translation reads as follows : " They had given their names to the army, and were at the same time fulfilling a cruel office, heeding the commands of the tyrant, and prepared to obey his commands, under the influence of fear. Suddenly—wonderful to believe are these things—they lay aside their madness, are converted and fly ; they desert the wicked camp of their leader, throw away their shields, military ornaments and blood-stained weapons. Confessing [the faith] they glory in bearing the triumphs of Christ [by martyrdom]. Believe [all ye who read] by [these verses of] Damasus what [marvels] the glory of Christ can effect."

Besides this inscription, there was found a marble column of the church, which had fallen into a lower gallery, and exhibited beneath the name ACILLEVS, a crown and a representation of his martyrdom. The base was also found of a similar column on which we may presume was a similar commemoration of Nereus.

In addition there was discovered, behind the apse of the church, a *cubiculum* evidently once held in high honor, and having on its walls a painting of *Petronella Mart.*—the place doubtless from which had been removed a sarcophagus bearing the inscription *Aureliæ Petronillæ Filiæ Dulcissimæ.* The painting shows the tradition of the locality. The name *Aureliæ Petronillæ* may also prove to be of signifi-

---

[1] Rom. Sott. I., p. 179.

cance ; and with other inscriptions—particularly one to Flavius Sabinus, another, *Aureliæ Cynacæ Conjugi*, and another,
Aureliæ Bonifatiæ Conjugi, etc.,—may be further indication of the early entrance of Christianity into some of the
nobler families in rank.   More important still, as indicating
a connection of the cemetery with Domitilla, are such
epitaphs as these : *Nutrix septem Liberorum Divi Vespa-
siäni et Flaviæ Domitillæ Vespasiani neptis* [Princeton
Rev., July, p. 269, year '54] ; *Filia Flaviæ Domitillæ
Vespasiani neptis Fecit Gluceræ*, etc. [Bull. di Arch. Crist.
1865, p. 23].   It is possible also that the fragment

RVM

ORVM,

on a stone with an anchor, should be restored to

SEPVLCRVM

FLAVIORVM,

though other restorations are possible.

    In a Bulletin published a year ago last March, and in
another received but a few weeks since, De Rossi describes
further discoveries in the neighborhood of the church of
Domitilla, and in the oldest portion of the cemetery.   "As
I send these pages to the press," remarks De Rossi, " there
is opening in the great necropolis of Domitilla, a chamber
adorned with paintings of classic type and very high antiquity.   They represent fantastic architectural designs, such
as one often sees at Pompeii, and little pastoral scenes.
There is no figure of the cycle peculiar to Christian art.
This chamber opens at the foot of a large staircase ; it is one
of the ancient and primitive nuclei of the cemetery of Domitilla.   Subsequently a vast subterranean region developed
starting from the staircase and having its centre in this
ancient chamber.   Thanks to a happy hit we are able to
assign to it its true name.   Among the ruins was found the
primitive title originally set in the middle of the wall oppo-
site the entrance ; the letters are of extraordinary size, of
remarkable beauty and of a classic type, which reminds

perhaps of the age of the Flavii, or of times but little poste-
rior :

AMPLIATI.

" In the lunette of a deep arcosolium excavated below
this inscription and apparently subsequent to it, we read, in
very beautiful letters of about the second century :

AVRELIAE · BONIFATIAE
CONIVGI · INCOMPARABILI
VERAE · CASTITATIS · FEMINAE
QVAE · VIXIT · ANN · XXV · M · II ·
DIEB · IIII · HOR · VI
AVREL · AMPLIATVS · CuM
GORDIANO · FILIO.

"The Aurelius Ampliatus who dedicated this monument to
his wife, is probably different from the Ampliatus founder
of the funeral chamber : perhaps his son. This chamber of
an Ampliatus and his posterity, the first and very ancient
nucleus of a vast region of the necropolis of Domitilla,
whose beginnings are contemporary with the apostolic age,
can it be a family monument of that Ampliatus to whom
St. Paul, in the Epistle to the Romans, addresses an affec-
tionate salutation? I [*Salute Ampliatus, my beloved in the
Lord.* Rom. xvi : 8]. The answer to a question so grave
naturally requires mature reflection as well as an exact
explanation, and complete examination of the entire
hypogeum."

In a later number of the Bulletin this question is taken
up anew, but is not brought to a conclusion.

The style of the decorations is again noticed and compared
with the frescoes of the house of Nero, of the house of Ger-
manicus on the Valentine, and of the villa Massomo, near
the baths of Diocletian. The fact is also developed that
Ampliatus was a cognomen of servants or of freedmen and
their descendants, and was never used of men of rank,
either pagan or Christian. It is all the more noticeable,
therefore, that a man of such origin or condition should

have so distinguished a monument, that in later times a staircase should be cut to open a way to his tomb, and that there should be many other indications of a place deemed worthy of special honor. There are marks in the chamber itself, not only of restorations, but of inscriptions subsequent to the first century. The cognomen *Bonifatia* was in use in the last half of the second century. De Rossi intimates a further discussion of the question in the forthcoming volume of his *Roma sotterranea*. For the present he declines to express an opinion as to the identification of this Ampliatus with the friend of the Apostle.[1]

Reviewing the evidence that has come to light, there can be no question that the cemetery of Domitilla is built in land which belonged to a branch of the Flavian family; that it began to assume a distinctively Christian character at least as early as the first half of the second century; that though possibly it began as the private burial-place of a family not yet converted to Christianity, there is no evidence of this; that the probability of the Christian character of Titus Flavius Clemens, and Flavia Domitilla his wife, gives plausibility to the supposition that from their time, and thus from the beginning, there were Christian interments in the cemetery which tradition names *Coemeterium Domitillæ;* and finally, that from the second, if not from the first century, it followed the general law of the Catacombs — the growth of private into public Christian cemeteries under the new, transforming and overmastering principle of Christian fraternity.

We have noticed thus far, only those cemeteries which learned men claim originated in the first century—finding but one that carries us back so far by any evidence as yet discovered, though there are several that in all probability were fully established and in use before Polycarp, the disciple of John,

---

[1] See *Bullet. di Arch. crist.* 1880, No. IV., p. 107, sq.; 1881, No. 2, p. 57, sq.; The *Athenaeum*, March 4, 1882, p. 289.

visited Rome and administered to the Church there the Sac-
rament of the Lord's Supper.

Were there time we would speak of several other cemeteries
—especially of those of Lucina, Practextatus, and Callistus,
which were doubtless all begun before the close of the
second century.

The opening of these long-lost places where the early
church administered its rites, sought refuge in persecution,
cherished its hope of a purer and immortal life, has naturally
turned a curious and eager attention to whatever their
pictured walls, or their epitaphs, can teach of the primitive
Christian faith.

It marks the progress of our age that Protestant scholars
gratefully acknowledge the learning and the integrity of the
Papal official, the Roman Catholic archæologist, who pre-
sides over the later fruitful investigations, and that he in
turn treats with respectful consideration the inquiries and
the criticisms of men of other communions. It is yet more
significant how many are interested in these inquiries, of all
schools of faith, who evidently are seeking, by the most
approved methods of historical and archæological study, to
find the truth. Certain canons of criticism seem to be com-
ing into light and acceptance, the results of patient and
thorough investigations, among which these are most promi-
nent :—(1) An art is not improvised. (2) The decoration of
the Christian tombs needs to be carefully studied in connection with that of the pagan, as well as with contemporary
literature. There is a realistic element common to both.
Much more was carried over from pagan to Christian life
than is sometimes appreciated. (3) The art of the Catacombs is not to be interpreted as a dogmatic hieroglyph,
designed to set forth in pictures the entire faith of the
Church, but is to be studied as a sepulchral art, limited by the
conditions and the motives which created it. A confessional
interpretation is sure to lead astray. The early Christian
art is manifestly not a perfect transcript of the creed of the

age which produced it. You cannot verify on its walls all the articles of so simple a creed as the old Roman form of the Apostles' Creed, which the later investigations show was probably in use at least as early as A. D. 140.

But if no one of us can find there all the articles of his creed, we may each obtain from it assurances and supports that none can afford to be without. There, in that realm of death, where symbols of sorrow and desolation might be expected on every hand, we see only the signs of a great deliverance, and the varied emblems of the power of a great Deliverer.

In the Catacombs of Callistus—which at the close of the second century came definitely under the control of the Church, and were superintended by one of its officers,—there is a series of six *cubicula*, which have received the name of *Chambers*, or *Chapels, of the Sacraments*. Three of them belong to the earlier period of the cemetery. From one the pictures are entirely gone. The other two preserve them,—retouched, doubtless—yet so that there is no good reason to question their early origin. Their interpretation has given rise to much discussion ; one sees in them this meaning, another that. But if we remember their location, if we go to them as men went who carried their dead thither, they all speak one language, the rescue of men from sin and death, the *resurrectio mortuorum* which a writer contemporary with their origin declares to be the *fiducia Christianorum*. Moses striking the rock, Baptism, a Fisherman, the paralytic carrying joyfully his bed, the deliverance of Isaac, the rescued mariners—Paul's fellow-voyagers, the parable of Jonah, the resurrection of Lazarus, the communion of disciples with the Risen One, the feast of the blessed,—this cycle of subjects, inexplicably meagre, if you are seeking for a system of faith, a *summa* of dogmas, is nevertheless full of rich suggestion and consolation to every mourner, as is that figure of the Good Shepherd which meets one everywhere as he wanders through these well-nigh interminable galleries, now in forms of almost classic grace and beauty in some decorated chamber, now in rudest scratches or black lines on some humblest grave,—the Shepherd who lays down his life, and leads through the shadows to green pastures and still waters.

Somehow in that old decaying Roman world men had learned that life may be rescued from all that would corrupt and destroy it, and be made forever free, joyful, victorious. How they learned the lesson, and the peace they found in it, is the burthen of the art of the Catacombs.

All of which is respectfully submitted.

For the Council,

EGBERT C. SMYTH.

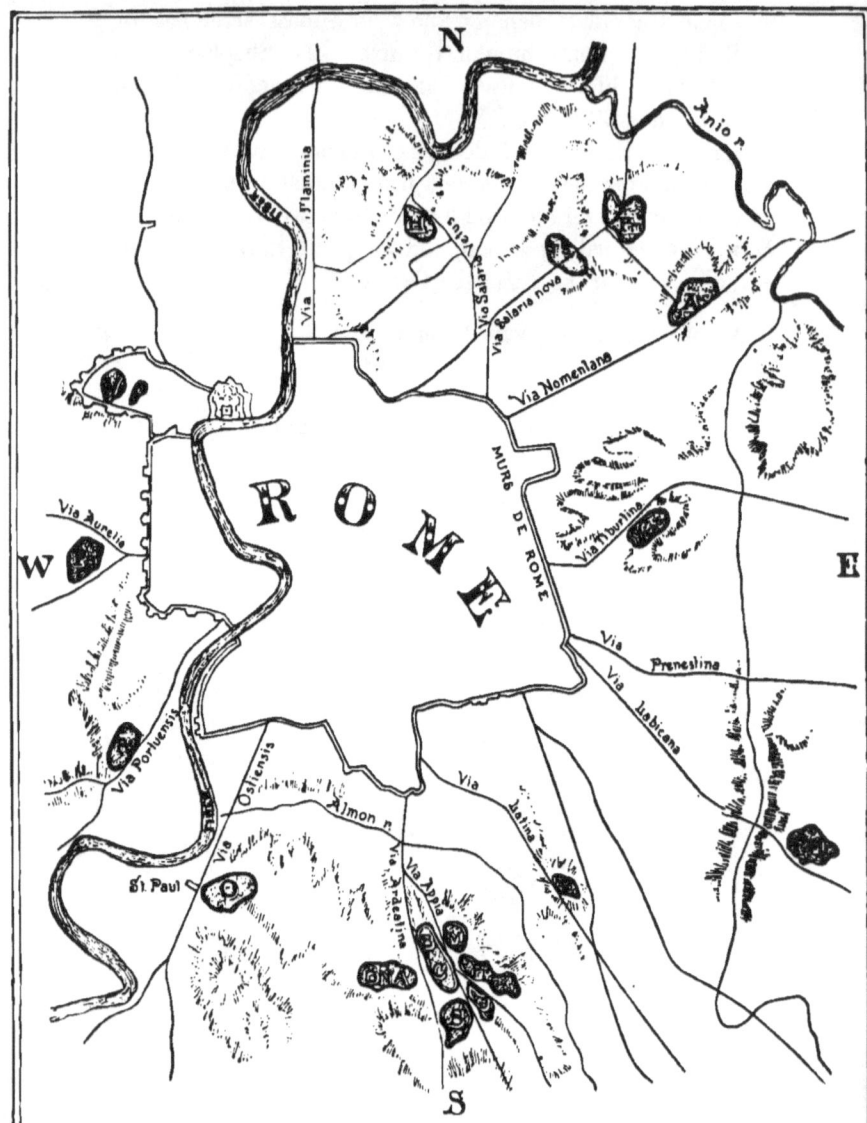

PLAN showing the location of the more important Catacombs.
FROM ROLLER.

KEY. H Cemetery of St. Hermes; Pri. Priscilla; T.S. Thrason, Saturninus;
A. Agnes; Cy. Cyriaca; P.M Peter, Marcellinus; L. Latin (closed); M. Maximus;
P. Pretextatus; J. Januarius; B. Balbina; C. Callixtus; S. Sebastian; DNA. Domi-
tilla, Nereus, Achilleus; O. Ostian; Po. Pontianus; Pa. Pancratius; V. Vatican.

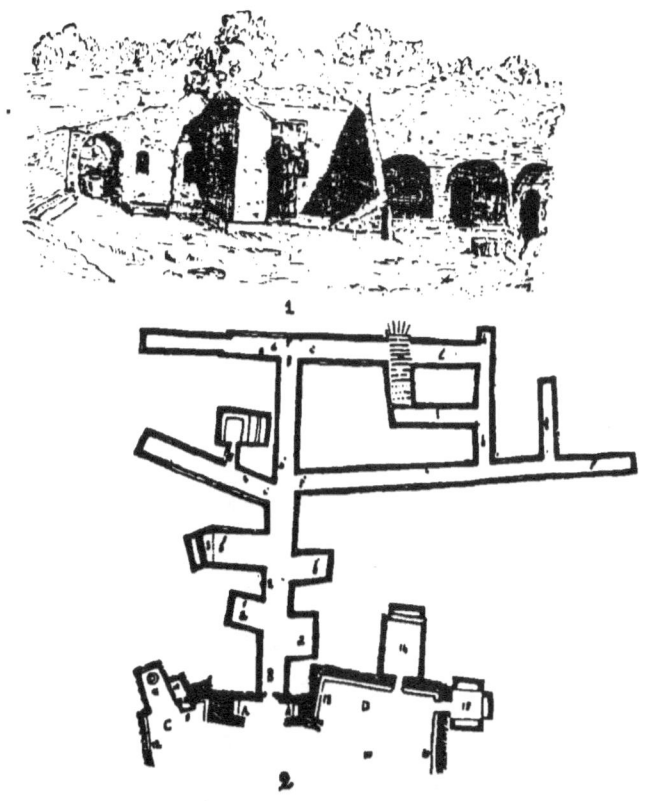

1.

2.

NOTE B., p. 20.

Figure 1 represents the original entrance to the catacomb of Domitilla described by Professor Mommsen. It was on a street, visible to any passer by. Figure 2 gives a plan of this vestibule with the adjoining *ambulacra*. The letters A A mark the Portico, where were found fragments of numerous sarcophagi of the second century, some perhaps as early as Trajan (A. D. 98); tiles dated A. D. 154, 142, 137, 123,—none later than A. D. 179; inscriptions in characters of the second century; the Christian symbol, an anchor; names of *Flavii, Claudii, Aurelii*, etc. B B mark the broad *ambulacrum* whose vaulted roof "is covered with the most exquisitely graceful designs, of the branches of a vine (with birds and winged genii among them) trailing with all the freedom of nature over the whole walls." The letters a a b b indicate recesses for sarcophagi; some of the figures mark the place of "the groups drawn on the side walls," referred to by Prof. Mommsen, viz., Daniel between two lions, 2; the Good Shepherd, 1; Noah's Ark, with the dove, 6; the Supper, 7. C. D., etc., mark constructions added probably in the third century. They indicate all the arrangements proper for a pagan tomb; the *custodia*, C; the *triclinium*, D; the *podia*, 12, 13, 16—thought to be for a bench or seat. C and D form an *atrium*, a *schola sodalium*, or place of reunion. 11 marks a well; 9 a cistern. For other details see Northcote & Brownlow, *Roma sott.*, I. p. 123 sq.; Roller, *Les Catacombs*, I. p. 58 sq.; and especially De Rossi, *Bullet. di arch. crist.* 1865, p. 33 sq., 41 sq.